MEALS ON THE GRILL
Made Easy

SIMPLE. SAVORY. DELICIOUS.

HAYSTACK MEDIA
SAN DIEGO, CA

Cover & Interior Design: Kayla Blanco

Photo Credit: Shutterstock 78875962; 40353577; 142550050; 70946950; 129448820; 91734476; 7890493; 180265259; 212755090; 119124010; 138543176; 210076219; 212292085; 110661035; 102851333

Published in the United States of America by

 **HAYSTACK MEDIA**
SAN DIEGO, CA

ISBN: 978-1-929862-01-6

10   9   8   7   6   5   4   3   2

TABLE OF CONTENTS

GRILLED RED HOT TRI-TIP BEEF

SERVES 6 TO 8

2½ - 3 lbs. tri-tip beef roast

¾ c. soy sauce

¾ c. red wine vinegar

¼ c. extra virgin olive oil

2 T. Dijon mustard

4 cloves garlic, minced

1 t. ground black pepper

3 habañero peppers, finely minced

4 Tabasco peppers, finely minced

Place the roast in a large self-sealing plastic bag. Add the remaining ingredients and seal tightly. Refrigerate for 12 to 24 hours. Grill as directed. To serve, slice thinly across the grain and place on a heated serving platter.

Grill over medium coals for 25 minutes. Turn, baste with the marinade and grill for 20 minutes, or until grilled as desired.

Preheat the grill for 10 to 15 minutes on high heat. Turn off 1 burner and reduce the heat to medium on the remaining burner(s). Place the roast over the burner that is turned off. Close the lid and grill until cooked to your preference, about 45 to 60 minutes.

TEX-MEX HAMBURGERS

SERVES 4

2 lbs. lean ground beef

¼ c. hickory-flavored barbecue sauce

½ yellow onion, chopped

2 T. salsa

1 t. chili powder

4 large sesame-seed hamburger buns, toasted

In a large bowl, combine the beef, sauce, onion, salsa and powder. Toss lightly to mix and shape into 4 patties. Grill as directed. To serve, place meat into the buns and add condiments.

Grill patties for 6 minutes over medium-hot coals. Turn and continue grilling to your preference.

Preheat the grill on medium-high for 10 to 15 minutes. Grill the meat for 10 minutes, turn and continue grilling for 4 to 6 minutes, or until cooked to your preference.

CHILI CILANTRO GRILLED BEEF

2 lbs. beef flank steak

¾ c. bottled chili sauce

½ c. canned beer

¼ c. vegetable oil

1 small, white onion, chopped

¼ c. fresh cilantro, chopped

¼ c. chili powder

½ t. ground cumin

½ t. salt

½ t. freshly ground black pepper

Place the steak in the bottom of a large, glass baking pan. Mix together the remaining ingredients and pour over the steak. Turn the steak to coat both sides. Cover tightly with plastic wrap and refrigerate for 4 to 12 hours, turning the steak occasionally. Discard the marinade and grill as directed. To serve, slice the steak very thinly across the grain and serve on a heated platter.

Grill over medium-low coals for 8 to 10 minutes. Turn once and grill for 7 minutes, or until grilled as desired.

Preheat the grill for 10 minutes on high heat. Sear the steak on each side for 2 minutes. Turn off 1 burner and lower the remaining burner(s) to medium. Move the steak over the burner that is off, close the lid and grill for 12 to 15 minutes, or until cooked to your preference.

GRILLING BEEF

SIRLOIN STEAKS
WITH ROSEMARY MUSTARD BUTTER

SERVES 6

6 sirloin steaks,
¾ to 1-inch thick

¼ c. butter

2 t. prepared
yellow mustard

1 t. ground paprika

1 T. fresh rosemary, finely
minced

1 t. salt

1 t. ground black pepper

Pat the steaks dry with paper toweling. Mix together the butter, mustard, paprika, rosemary, salt and pepper. Blend well. Place equal amounts of the butter on one side of each steak and smooth over the steaks evenly. Grill as directed.

Grill over medium coals, buttered side facing up, for 7 minutes. Turn and grill for 5 to 7 minutes, or until cooked as desired.

Preheat the grill for 10 to 15 minutes on high heat. Place the steaks on the grill and sear them for 1 minute. Turn 1 burner off and turn the remaining burner(s) to medium. Place the steaks over the burner that is off. Close the lid and grill for 14 to 16 minutes, or until cooked to your preference.

SOY GARLIC BEEF TENDERLOIN

SERVES 6

1½ to 2 lbs. beef tenderloin steak

½ c. pineapple-orange juice

2 T. lime juice

¼ c. soy sauce

1 t. cayenne pepper

1 t. garlic powder

1 t. chili powder

¼ t. sugar

Place the steak in a large glass pan and cover with the juices and soy sauce. Wrap and refrigerate for 30 minutes or up to 1 hour. Mix together the cayenne pepper and remaining ingredients. Just before grilling, sprinkle the steak with the spices. Grill as directed.

Grill over medium coals for 7 minutes. Turn and grill for 5 to 7 minutes, or until cooked as desired.

Preheat the grill for 10 minutes on high heat. Place the steak on the grill and sear it for 2 minutes. Turn off 1 burner and reduce the heat to medium on the remaining burner(s). Place the steak over the burner that is off. Close the lid and grill for 14 minutes, or until cooked to your preference.

BOURBON-BARBECUED NEW YORK STEAKS

SERVES 4

The hearty bite of bourbon brings out the best of this beef.

1½ lbs. New York beef steak, cut into 4 portions

½ c. dark brown sugar

½ c. bourbon whiskey

Pat the steaks dry and use a sharp knife to score each steak lightly across the top. Just prior to grilling, make a paste of the whiskey and sugar. Smooth evenly on the steaks. Grill as directed.

Place the steaks on the grill with the sugar and bourbon paste on the top. Grill over medium coals for 7 minutes. Drizzle additional bourbon over each steak as it grills. Turn once and grill for 5 to 7 minutes.

Preheat the grill for 10 to 15 minutes on high heat. Place the steaks with the whiskey paste on top on the grill and sear for 1 minute. Turn 1 burner off and reduce the heat to medium on the remaining burner(s). Turn the steaks and place over the burner that is off. Close the lid and grill for 13 to 17 minutes, or until cooked to your preference.

HONEY MUSTARD BEEF HANGAR STEAK

SERVES 4

2 T. dry mustard

2 T. honey

pinch salt

pinch white pepper

1 T. white wine vinegar

½ t. cornstarch

½ c. homemade or prepared mayonnaise

1½ lbs. beef hangar steaks, cut into 4 portions

Combine in a small saucepan the mustard, honey, salt, pepper and vinegar. Blend until smooth. Add the cornstarch and heat over low heat until thickened and smooth, stirring constantly. Remove from the heat and cool for fifteen minutes. Whisk in the mayonnaise and blend thoroughly. Grill the steak as directed. To serve, slice the beef in thin slices and pour the sauce over each serving.

Grill the beef over medium coals for 5 to 6 minutes. Turn and grill for 4 to 5 minutes, or until grilled as desired.

Preheat the grill for 10 to 15 minutes on high heat. Place the steaks on the grill and sear for 2 minutes on one side. Turn the beef. Turn 1 burner off and reduce the heat to medium on the remaining burner(s). Place the steaks over the burner that is off. Close the lid and grill for 5 to 7 minutes, or until cooked to your preference.

RIBEYE STEAKS
WITH BALSAMIC HERB MARINADE

SERVES 4

4 beef ribeye steaks, about ¾-inch thick

¼ c. extra virgin olive oil

1 T. balsamic vinegar

½ t. Worcestershire sauce

1 clove garlic, minced

1 t. fresh basil, minced

1 t. fresh thyme, minced

1 t. fresh parsley, minced

1 t. ground black pepper

Place the steaks in a large, self-sealing plastic bag. Add the remaining ingredients and seal tightly. Refrigerate for 4 to 12 hours, turning the bag occasionally. Discard the marinade and grill as directed.

Grill the steaks over medium coals for 7 minutes. Turn and grill for 7 to 9 minutes, or until cooked as desired.

Preheat the grill for 10 to 15 minutes on high heat. Place the steaks on the grill and sear on high heat for 1 minute. Turn 1 burner off and reduce the heat to medium on the remaining burner(s). Turn the steaks and place them over the burner that is off. Close the lid and grill for 13 to 18 minutes, or until cooked to your preference.

RED PEPPER & SHALLOT BEEF KEBOBS

SERVES 6

1½ - 2 lbs. beef skirt steak, unrolled, cut into 6 portions

3 T. red wine vinegar

½ c. extra virgin olive oil

1 t. salt

1 t. ground black pepper

1 t. dry mustard

6 shallots, peeled, quartered

2 red bell peppers, cut into large pieces

6 10-inch bamboo skewers, soaked in water

Place the strips of steak in a large, self-sealing plastic bag. Add the vinegar, oil, salt, pepper and mustard and mix in the bag with the steak. Refrigerate for one hour. Discard the marinade, reserving one-fourth cup. Thread the beef onto the skewers, alternating wrapping the beef over and around the shallots and red pepper pieces on each skewer. Grill as directed.

Grill the kebobs over medium coals for 6 minutes. Turn and baste with the reserved marinade. Grill for 6 to 8 minutes, or until grilled as desired.

Preheat the grill for 10 to 15 minutes on high heat. Turn the burners to medium, place the skewers on the grill and cook for about 14 to 16 minutes, turning once or twice.

ROASTED GREEN CHILE SIRLOIN BURGERS

SERVES 4

½ c. purple onion, finely chopped

3 T. roasted green chilies, chopped

1 t. salt

1 t. ground black pepper

¼ t. Tabasco® sauce

1½ lbs. ground sirloin beef

Combine all of the ingredients except the beef in a medium bowl and toss to mix well. Add the beef and gently toss for two minutes with the other ingredients. Do not over-mix. Lightly pat the beef into four patties, each about ¾ to 1-inch thick. Grill as directed. Serve on toasted sourdough bread with your choice of condiments.

Grill over medium coals for 4 minutes. Turn once and grill for 5 to 6 minutes, or until grilled as desired.

Preheat the grill for 15 minutes on high heat. Turn all burners to medium and grill the burgers over the burners for 5 to 6 minutes on each side, or until cooked as desired. Turn the burgers once while grilling.

GRILLED LEMON HERB TOP SIRLOIN

SERVES 4 TO 5

1½ lbs. beef top sirloin

½ c. canola oil

¼ c. soy sauce

¼ c. Worcestershire sauce

¼ c. fresh lemon juice

1 t. dry mustard

1 t. salt

1 t. ground black pepper

2 T. fresh parsley, minced

2 cloves garlic, minced

Place the beef in a large, self-sealing plastic bag. Add the remaining ingredients and mix well. Refrigerate overnight. Discard the marinade and grill as directed.

Grill the sirloin over medium coals for 6 minutes. Turn and grill for 7 to 9 minutes, or until grilled as desired.

Preheat the grill for 10 to 15 minutes on high heat. Place the sirloin grill and sear it for 2 minutes. Turn 1 burner off and reduce the heat to medium on the remaining burner(s). Turn the sirloin and place over the burner that is off. Close the lid and grill for 12 to 19 minutes, or until cooked to your preference.

KANSAS CITY RUBBED BEEF TENDERLOIN

SERVES 6

2 lbs. beef tenderloin, cut into 6 portions

¼ c. sugar

2 T. salt

1 T. ground paprika

1 t. cayenne pepper

2 t. chili powder

1 t. ground cumin

Place the beef on a flat surface. Mix the remaining ingredients together in a small plastic bag. Rub the spices into each side of the tenderloin pieces, pressing lightly to adhere. Grill as directed.

Grill the tenderloin over medium coals for 6 minutes. Turn and grill for 5 to 7 minutes, or until grilled to your preference.

Preheat the grill for 10 to 15 minutes on high heat. Place the steaks on the grill and sear for 1 minute. Turn 1 burner off and turn the remaining burner(s) to medium. Turn the steaks and place over the burner that is off. Close the lid and grill for 12 to 14 minutes, or until cooked to your preference.

STEAK & SALSA MUSHROOMS

3 T. butter or margarine, softened

1 clove garlic, minced

7 oz. can green chilies, chopped

1 T. fresh cilantro, chopped

2 c. fresh mushrooms, cleaned and sliced

2 T. prepared salsa

1 t. freshly ground black pepper

4 beef sirloin steaks, ¾-1 inch thick

Line a shallow bowl with heavy duty aluminum foil, allowing the foil to extend two or three inches past the rim of the bowl. Place all ingredients except the steaks in the bowl and mix lightly. Fold and seal all foil edges tightly. Set aside. Grill the steaks and vegetables as directed.

Heat the coals to medium heat. Scatter the coals slightly in a circle and place the foil packet of vegetables directly in the middle of the coals. Place the steaks on the rack above, positioning each over coals. Grill the steaks for 6 minutes. Turn and grill for 6 to 7 minutes, or until grilled as desired. Using heavy-duty oven mitts, remove the steaks and vegetables from the grill. Spoon the vegetables and sauce over each steak.

Preheat the grill for 10 to 15 minutes on high heat. Sear the steaks for 1 minute. Turn 1 burner off and reduce the heat to medium on the remaining burner(s). Turn the steaks and place over the burner that is off. Add the foil packet and close the lid. Grill for 13 to 17 minutes, or until cooked to your preference. Serve the mushrooms and sauce over the steaks.

PEPPER-CRUSTED LONDON BROIL
WITH FRESH TOMATO RELISH

3 large ripe tomatoes, chopped

2 cloves garlic, minced

1 c. canned or frozen, thawed whole kernel corn

1 small, white onion, chopped

2 t. fresh cilantro, minced

1 T. tomato sauce

½ t. ground black pepper

1 t. salt

1½ to 2 lbs. beef London broil, 1½ to 2 inches thick

2 to 3 T. cracked black peppercorns

Place the tomatoes, garlic, corn, onion and cilantro in a food processor and pulse once or twice briefly. Do not over-mix. Place the vegetables in a medium bowl and add the tomato sauce, pepper and salt. Mix lightly and chill.

Press the peppercorns over the surface of the steak. Grill as directed. Slice thinly and serve the tomato relish on the side.

Grill over medium coals for 8 minutes. Turn and continue grilling for 7 to 10 minutes, or according to your preference. The beef should be rare to medium for best results.

Preheat the grill for 15 minutes on high heat. Grill for 4 minutes. Turn 1 burner off and turn the remaining burner(s) to medium. Turn the steak and move over the burner that is off. Close the lid and grill the steak for 13 to 15 minutes, turning once.

GRILLING BEEF

BLUE RIBBON BARBECUED BEEF RIBS

SERVES 4

1 T. vegetable oil

1 purple onion, finely diced

8 oz. can tomato sauce

½ c. dark brown sugar

¼ c. apple cider vinegar

2 T. Worcestershire sauce

¼ c. chili powder

1 t. salt

½ t. dry mustard

4 lbs. beef ribs, trimmed of excess fat

Sauté the onion for two to three minutes in the oil in a medium saucepan. Add the remaining ingredients, except the ribs. Blend well and cook over medium-high heat until the sauce boils. Reduce the heat; simmer for 15 minutes. Grill as directed, basting the ribs with the sauce. If desired, reheat the remaining sauce to boiling, simmer for 5 minutes and use at the table.

Grill the ribs over medium coals for 4 minutes. Turn and sear the other side of the ribs for 2 minutes. Turn again and baste with the sauce, grilling for 6 minutes. Turn, baste and grill for 3 to 5 minutes. Test for doneness and continue basting and grilling until the ribs are cooked as desired, 1 to 1 1/2 hours.

Preheat the grill for 10 to 15 minutes on high heat. Turn 1 burner off and reduce the heat to medium on the remaining burners. Place the ribs over the burner that is off. Close the lid and grill for about 50 to 60 minutes, turning the ribs and basting with the sauce occasionally.

ASIAN CHILI SAUCE FLANK STEAK

SERVES 4 to 6

1½ lbs. beef flank steak

¾ c. canola oil

¼ c. soy sauce

¼ c. honey

2 green onions, minced

2 cloves garlic, minced

1 t. ground ginger

1 t. Asian chili sauce

1 t. ground black pepper

Score the flank steak lightly in a two-inch diamond pattern. Place the remaining ingredients in a self-sealing plastic bag and mix well. Add the beef and refrigerate for 4 to 12 hours. Discard the marinade and grill as directed. To serve, slice thinly across the grain of the meat.

Grill the steak over medium coals for 8 minutes. Turn and grill for 8 to 10 minutes, or until cooked as desired.

Preheat the grill for 10 to 15 minutes on high heat. Sear the steak on each side for 2 minutes. Turn off 1 burner and reduce the heat on the remaining burners to medium. Move the steak over the burner that is off, close the lid and grill for 12 to 14 minutes, or until cooked to your preference.

HOT & HONEYED PORK RIBS

SERVES 4 to 6

3 lbs. pork ribs

¼ c. jalapeño chile peppers, finely minced

½ c. soy sauce

2 c. prepared mild salsa

2 cloves garlic, minced

½ c. honey

Parboil the ribs by placing them in a stockpot of boiling water. Reduce the heat and simmer for 1 hour. Remove the ribs, place in a shallow glass baking dish. Mix together the chile pepper, soy sauce, salsa, garlic and honey and pour the sauce over the ribs. Cover with plastic wrap and refrigerate for at least one hour or up to twelve hours. Turn the ribs occasionally in the marinade. Discard the marinade and grill as directed.

Grill the ribs over medium coals for 10 minutes. Turn and grill for 12 to 15 minutes, or until cooked through.

Preheat the grill for 10 to 15 minutes on high heat. Reduce the heat to low and grill for 20 to 30 minutes until cooked through, basting occasionally.

FIVE-SPICE PORK TENDERLOIN

SERVES 4

¼ c. sugar

3 T. soy sauce

2 T. fish sauce

2 T. miso

½ t. Chinese five-spice powder

¼ t. salt

1½ to 2 lbs. pork tenderloin

Combine the sugar, soy sauce, fish sauce, miso, Chinese powder and salt in a large, self-sealing plastic bag. Add the tenderloin and marinate 4 hours or overnight. Turn the bag frequently. Grill as directed.

Grill the tenderloin over medium coals for 3 minutes, turning to sear each side. Move the coals to the sides of the grill so that they are not directly under the pork and allow the meat to grill for 25 to 30 minutes, or to your preference. Brush the marinade over the pork once or twice while grilling. Remove the tenderloin and slice to serve.

Preheat the grill for 10 to 15 minutes on high heat. Turn off 1 burner and reduce the heat on the remaining burners to medium. Place the tenderloin over the burner that is off, close the lid and grill for 25 to 35 minutes, turning once.

PORK CHOPS IN MIDNIGHT MARINADE

SERVES 4

3 T. Worcestershire sauce

½ c. dry white wine

2 T. extra virgin olive oil

1 t. salt

1 t. ground black pepper

2 t. hot chili sauce

1 T. apple cider vinegar

3 T. soy sauce

¼ c. dark brown sugar

4 pork loin chops, 6 to 8 oz. each

Combine all of the ingredients except for the pork chops in a large, self-sealing plastic bag. Mix thoroughly. Add the pork and marinate in the refrigerator for 2 hours or up to 12 hours. Remove the chops from the bag and grill as directed.

Grill the chops over medium coals for 5 to 6 minutes. Turn and baste with the marinade. Grill for 8 to 10 minutes, or until cooked to your preference.

Preheat the grill for 10 to 15 minutes on high heat. Turn off 1 burner and turn the remaining burner(s) to medium. Place the chops on the burner that is off and grill for 15 to 20 minutes, or according to your preference.

HONEY LIME PORK LOIN CHOPS

SERVES 6

6 pork loin chops, 6 to 8 oz. each

3 T. Dijon mustard

¼ c. honey

2 T. lime juice

¼ c. canola oil

¼ t. salt

1 t. ground pepper

1 T. fresh parsley, minced

Place the pork chops in a large, self-sealing plastic bag. Add the remaining ingredients and mix well, covering the chops completely. Refrigerate for four hours or up to twelve hours, turning the bag occasionally to coat the chops completely. Grill as desired.

Grill the chops over medium-hot coals for 2 minutes. Turn and grill for 1 minute. Scatter the coals to reduce the heat and grill the chops for 8 minutes. Turn and grill for 8 to 12 minutes, or cooked according to your preference.

Preheat the grill for 10 to 15 minutes on high heat. Turn off 1 burner and turn the remaining burner(s) to medium. Place the chops on the burner that is off and grill for 15 to 20 minutes, or according to your preference.

CORIANDER & LEMON GREEK KEBOBS

SERVES 6 TO 8

¼ c. fresh lemon juice

½ c. extra virgin olive oil

2 T. onion, finely minced

2 cloves garlic, finely minced

1 t. ground coriander

½ t. ground cumin

½ t. cayenne pepper

⅛ t. ground ginger

⅛ t. ground allspice

2 lbs. boneless pork, cut into 1-inch cubes

8 metal or bamboo skewers

Combine the seasonings and herbs and mix well. Place in a self-sealing bag and add the pork. Refrigerate for 2 hours or up to 12 hours. Discard the marinade and thread the pork onto the skewers. Grill as directed.

Grill the kebobs over medium coals for 5 minutes. Turn and grill for 5 minutes. Turn and grill the kebobs for 5 to 8 minutes, until cooked to your preference.

Preheat the grill for 10 to 15 minutes on high heat. Turn 1 burner off and turn the remaining burner(s) to medium. Place the kebobs over the burner that is off. Close the lid and grill for 15 to 20 minutes, turning the skewers once.

SMOKIN' HOT RUBBED PORK LOIN CHOPS

SERVES 6

½ c. dark brown sugar, packed

¼ t. cayenne pepper

¼ t. ground cinnamon

½ t. garlic salt

1 T. ground black pepper

1 T. chili powder

1 T. ground paprika

6 boneless pork loin chops,
cut 1 to 1½ inches thick

Combine the seasonings and mix well. Place the chops in a glass baking pan and generously dust with the rub. Press the rub generously into both sides of each chop. Cover tightly with plastic wrap and refrigerate for 1 hour or up to 12 hours. Grill as directed.

Grill over medium coals for 3 minutes. Turn and grill for 3 minutes. Move the coals away from direct heat and continue grilling the chops for 12 to 20 minutes, or until cooked to your preference.

Preheat the grill for 10 to 15 minutes on high heat. Turn off 1 burner and turn the remaining burner(s) to medium. Place the chops on the burner that is off and grill for 20 minutes, or according to your preference.

GAZPACHO PORK CHOPS
WITH GRILLED CORN SALSA

SERVES 4

4 pork loin chops

2 T. tomato sauce

¼ c. extra virgin olive oil

1 t. ground black pepper

½ t. salt

1 T. fresh cilantro, chopped

2 cloves garlic, minced

Grilled Corn Salsa

2 large ears corn, husks removed

2 medium tomatoes, chopped

3 T. white onion, chopped

¼ c. green pepper, chopped

2 cloves garlic, chopped

2 T. fresh cilantro, chopped

1 t. salt

½ t. ground black pepper

Place the pork in a large, self-sealing plastic bag. Add the remaining marinade ingredients and refrigerate for 1 hour or up to 12 hours. Grill as directed and serve with the *Grilled Corn Salsa*.

To prepare the *Grilled Corn Salsa*, place 2 tablespoons of butter on each of 2 large squares of foil. Add the corn and sprinkle each ear with seasoned salt. Wrap the corn tightly and place in the coals of the barbecue. Grill for 6 minutes. Turn and grill for 5 to 6 minutes. Remove and cut the corn from the cobs. Place the corn in a serving bowl and toss with the tomatoes, onion, pepper, garlic, cilantro, salt and pepper.

Grill the pork chops over medium coals for 5 minutes. Turn and baste with the marinade. Grill for 7 to 10 minutes, or until cooked to your preference.

MEDITERRANEAN LAMB BURGERS

SERVES 6

2 lbs. ground lamb

½ c. sweet onion, minced

4 cloves garlic, minced

¼ c. fresh cilantro, minced

½ t. ground cinnamon

½ t. ground paprika

½ t. ground cumin

½ t. ground coriander

½ t. chili powder

3 whole wheat pita rounds, cut in half

3 c. romaine lettuce, shredded

¼ c. sour cream

6 slices sweet purple onion

6 slices ripe tomato

Place the lamb in a large mixing bowl and lightly toss with your fingertips. Add the seasonings and toss lightly. Do not over-work the meat. Shape into 6 patties and grill as directed. Place 1 grilled patty in each pita half and arrange the lettuce, sour cream, onion and tomato on top.

Grill the lamb over hot coals for 5 minutes. Turn and grill for 4 to 6 minutes, or until cooked to your preference. Do not handle the meat more than is necessary.

Preheat the grill for 15 minutes on high heat. Turn all burners to high and grill the burgers for 4 to 5 minutes on each side, or until cooked as desired. Turn the burgers once while grilling. Do not handle the meat more than is necessary.

LEMON BUTTERFLIED LEG OF LAMB

SERVES 6 TO 8

4 to 6 lbs. leg of lamb, boned, butterflied

2 T. fresh lemon juice

¼ c. extra virgin olive oil

¾ c. dry white wine

6 whole dried bay leaves

1 white onion, chopped

4 cloves garlic, minced

½ t. lemon peel, finely minced

1 t. fresh oregano, finely minced

Place the leg of lamb in a large glass baking dish, pressing lightly to flatten it as much as possible. Combine the remaining ingredients and pour over the lamb. Refrigerate 4 hours or overnight. Grill as directed.

Grill over medium-hot coals for 2 minutes. Turn and grill for 2 minutes to completely sear the meat. Cover and grill for about 1½ hours, or until it is 160°F for medium, or until cooked to your preference. Baste occasionally with the marinade. Let stand for 5 to 10 minutes prior to carving.

Preheat the grill for 10 to 15 minutes on high heat. Grill the lamb for 5 minutes on high heat, turn and grill for 5 minutes. Reduce the heat to medium. Close the lid and grill for about 2 hours, basting often until it is 160°F for medium-well. Let stand for 5 to 10 minutes prior to carving.

MOROCCAN LAMB SHISH KEBOBS

1½ to 2 lbs. boneless lamb, cut into 1-inch cubes

¼ c. soy sauce

½ c. vegetable oil

2 green onions, minced

2 cloves garlic, minced

1 t. ground ginger

¼ c. honey

8 long metal or bamboo skewers

8 crimini mushrooms, cleaned and cut in half

1 orange pepper, cut into large squares

1 white onion, cut into large squares

Place the lamb in a self-sealing plastic bag. Add the soy sauce, oil, green onions, garlic, ginger and honey and refrigerate for 4 hours. Thread the vegetables and lamb on each skewer, alternating each and grill as directed.

Grill the kebobs over medium-hot coals for 2 minutes. Turn and grill for 2 minutes to seal in the juices. Cover and grill for 14 to 15 minutes or until the lamb is cooked as desired.

Preheat the grill for 10 to 15 minutes on high heat. Reduce the heat to medium, place the skewers on the grill and cook for about 15 to 20 minutes, turning once or twice.

GRILLING PORK & LAMB

GARLIC & ROSEMARY
BUTTERFLIED LEG OF LAMB

SERVES 6 TO 8

4 to 6 lbs. leg of lamb, boned, butterflied

6 cloves garlic, cut into very thin slices

1 T. dried rosemary, crushed

1 t. salt

1 t. freshly ground black pepper

Place the lamb on a large working surface. With the tip of a very sharp knife, make several small slits over the entire leg of lamb. Insert the slices of garlic into the small pockets. Sprinkle the rosemary into the leg of lamb, pressing slightly with your fingertips. Sprinkle the salt and pepper over the leg of lamb. Grill as directed.

Grill over medium-hot coals for 2 minutes. Turn and grill for 2 minutes to completely sear the meat. Cover and grill for about 1½ hours or until the meat is 160°F for medium-well, or until cooked to your preference. Allow the lamb to stand for 5 to 10 minutes prior to carving.

Preheat the grill for 10 to 15 minutes on high heat. Grill the lamb for 5 minutes on high heat, turn and grill for 5 minutes. Reduce the heat to medium. Close the lid and grill for about 2 hours or until the meat is 160°F for medium-well. Let stand for 5 to 10 minutes prior to carving.

SPICY SWEET RUBBED LAMB CHOPS

SERVES 4

12 lamb rib chops
(about 4 ounces each)

2 T. dark brown sugar

2 t. crushed red pepper

½ t. ground cumin

1 t. garlic powder

1 t. ground black pepper

Place the chops on a flat surface. Combine the remaining ingredients in a small bowl. Press the rub into each chop, covering as much of each chop as possible on both sides with the rub. Grill as directed.

Grill over medium-hot coals for 3 minutes. Turn and grill for 5 to 8 minutes, or until cooked as desired.

Preheat the grill for 10 to 15 minutes on high heat. Turn off 1 burner and reduce the remaining burner(s) to medium. Place the chops on the grill and cook for 10 to 15 minutes. Turn once while grilling.

CHILE TEQUILA LAMB KEBOBS

SERVES 5

2 lbs. boneless lamb, cut into 1-inch pieces

¼ c. premium tequila

2 red chilies, seeded and minced

2 ripe tomatoes, chopped

1 small purple onion, chopped

½ c. orange juice

1 T. brown sugar

1 t. salt

1 t. ground black pepper

¼ c. extra virgin olive oil

10 long metal or bamboo skewers

Place the lamb in a self-sealing plastic bag. Add the remaining ingredients and mix thoroughly. Refrigerate for 2 hours or up to 12 hours. Thread the lamb onto each skewer, alternating pieces with the vegetables. Grill as directed.

Grill the lamb kebobs over medium-hot coals for 4 minutes, covered. Turn the kebobs and baste with the marinade. Grill for 5 to 6 minutes. Turn and baste again a few more times until the lamb is cooked to your preference and the marinade is absorbed into the meat.

Preheat the grill for 10 to 15 minutes with all burners on high. Turn the burners to medium, place the skewers on the grill and cook for about 15 to 20 minutes, turning once or twice.

GARLIC GLAZED LAMB CHOPS

SERVES 6

A sweet and rich molasses glaze enhances these chops.

1 c. dark molasses

2 t. dry mustard

2 T. apple cider vinegar

3 cloves garlic, minced

6 lamb loin chops

Mix together in a small bowl the molasses, mustard, vinegar and garlic. Grill the chops as directed.

Place the chops on the grill over medium-hot coals. Liberally brush with the sauce. Grill for 5 minutes and turn the chops. Brush with the sauce again and grill for 3 minutes. Turn again, brush the chops with sauce and grill for 2 minutes. Turn the chops for the last time, brush with sauce and grill for 2 minutes.

Preheat the grill for 10 to 15 minutes on high heat. Reduce the heat on each burner to medium and place the chops on the grill. Brush with the sauce and grill for 5 minutes. Turn and brush with the sauce again. Grill for 5 to 7 minutes, turning once.

LIME CHICKEN SATAY
WITH WARM PEANUT SAUCE

SERVES 6

6 boneless chicken breasts, sliced into strips

2 T. dark brown sugar

2 t. curry powder

2 T. creamy peanut butter

½ c. soy sauce

½ c. lime juice

3 cloves garlic, minced

pinch chili powder

12 to 16 short skewers

Warm Peanut Sauce

1 c. creamy peanut butter

½ c. coconut milk

2 T. lime juice

2 T. soy sauce

1 t. ground ginger

2 cloves garlic, minced

Place the chicken in a self-sealing plastic bag. Add the sugar, curry powder, peanut butter, soy sauce, juice, garlic and chili powder. Mix together and refrigerate for 4 to 6 hours. Remove the chicken from the marinade and thread the chicken onto the skewers. Grill as directed. Serve with the *Warm Peanut Sauce.*

Combine the ingredients for the sauce in a saucepan and cook over low heat for 2 to 3 minutes. Heat and stir until the sauce is warm throughout.

Grill the chicken skewers over hot coals for 8 minutes. Turn and grill for 7 to 10 minutes, or until cooked through completely.

Preheat the grill for 10 to 15 minutes on high heat. Reduce the heat to medium and grill the chicken skewers for 15 to 20 minutes, or until cooked through completely.

BUFFALO BILL'S GRILLED CHICKEN

SERVES 8

2 8 oz. cans tomato sauce

½ c. cider vinegar

¼ c. prepared mustard

¼ c. dark brown sugar

½ c. onion, chopped

3 cloves garlic, minced

1 t. freshly ground black pepper

8 boneless, skinless chicken breast halves

Combine all ingredients except the chicken in a medium bowl. Whisk and stir to blend. Grill the chicken as directed, basting often with the sauce.

Grill the chicken over hot coals for 6 minutes. Turn and baste with the sauce. Continue grilling for 6 to 8 minutes, or until the chicken is cooked through completely.

Preheat the grill for 10 to 15 minutes on high heat. Reduce the heat to medium and grill the chicken for 12 to 14 minutes, basting frequently, until cooked through completely.

GARLICKY LIME CHICKEN THIGHS

SERVES 4

½ c. fresh lime juice

3 cloves garlic, minced

¼ c. canola oil

2 T. fresh cilantro, chopped

2 green onions, thinly sliced

1 t. ground ginger

2 t. chili powder

8 boneless, skinless chicken thighs

Mix together the juice, garlic, oil, cilantro, onions, ginger and chili powder in a self-sealing plastic bag. Add the thighs and refrigerate for 4 hours or up to overnight. Grill as directed.

Grill the chicken thighs over hot coals for 6 minutes. Turn and baste with the marinade. Grill for 6 to 8 minutes, or until completely cooked through.

Preheat the grill for 10 to 15 minutes on high heat. Reduce the heat to medium and add the thighs. Close the lid and grill for 12 to 14 minutes, or until cooked completely through. Baste occasionally while grilling.

SAVORY LEMON CHICKEN BREASTS

SERVES 8

8 boneless chicken breasts

½ c. fresh lemon juice

4 cloves garlic, minced

¼ c. vegetable oil

2 t. fresh tarragon, minced

2 t. fresh marjoram, minced

1 t. freshly ground black
pepper

1 t. salt

Place the chicken in a large glass pan. Mix together the remaining ingredients and pour over the chicken. Cover with plastic wrap and refrigerate for 6 hours or up to 12 hours. Turn the chicken breasts once or twice. Grill as directed.

Grill the chicken over hot coals for 6 minutes. Turn and baste with the marinade. Continue grilling for 6 to 8 minutes, or until the chicken is cooked through completely.

Preheat the grill for 10 to 15 minutes on high heat. Reduce the heat to medium and grill the chicken for 12 to 14 minutes, basting often, until cooked through completely.

ZINGY HOT BBQ CHICKEN WINGS

SERVES 4 TO 6

2 lbs. chicken wings

½ c. soy sauce

2 T. hoisin sauce

2 T. chili sauce

¼ c. honey

¼ c. vinegar

3 cloves garlic, minced

½ t. chili powder

½ t. freshly ground black pepper

Place the chicken wings in a large glass pan. Mix together the remaining ingredients and cover the wings evenly. Wrap tightly with plastic wrap and refrigerate for 2 hours or up to 12 hours. Grill as directed.

Grill the wings over medium coals for 6 minutes. Turn and close the grill. Grill for 10 minutes, or until cooked completely through.

Preheat the grill on high heat for 10 to 15 minutes. Reduce the heat to medium and grill the wings for 20 to 25 minutes, or until cooked through completely.

CARIBBEAN JERK CHICKEN SKEWERS

SERVES 6

1 c. canola oil

4 cloves garlic, roughly chopped

1 large purple onion, roughly chopped

2 habañero peppers, seeded and chopped

2 T. fresh parsley, chopped

¼ c. cider vinegar

¼ c. dark brown sugar, packed

¼ t. ground cinnamon

⅛ t. ground cloves

1½ t. ground allspice

¼ c. fresh lime juice

2 lbs. chicken breast, cut into 1-inch cubes

12 skewers

Combine all of the ingredients except the chicken and process in a blender for 2 minutes, or until smooth. Thread the chicken onto the skewers and place in a glass pan. Pour the sauce over the chicken. Cover tightly and marinate in therefrigerator for at least 2 hours or up to overnight. Grill as directed.

Grill the chicken over hot coals for 10 minutes. Turn and grill for 6 to 8 minutes, or until the chicken is completely cooked through.

Preheat the grill for 10 to 15 minutes on high heat. Reduce the heat to medium and grill the skewers for 10 minutes. Turn the chicken, close the lid and grill for another 6 to 8 minutes, or until the chicken is cooked through completely.

SICILIAN GRILLED CHICKEN & GARLIC

SERVES 4

3 to 4 lbs. roasting chicken, backbone split and wing tips removed

2 t. ground oregano

2 t. salt

2 t. freshly ground black pepper

4 cloves garlic, finely minced

Place the chicken in a large glass pan, pressing down to flatten it as much as possible. Mix together the oregano, salt, pepper and garlic; rub over the chicken, pressing lightly. Cover tightly with plastic wrap and refrigerate for 1 hour or up to 4 hours. Grill as directed.

Grill the chicken over medium-low coals for 40 to 50minutes. Turn the chicken every 15 minutes. When the chicken is completely cooked through, remove to a cutting board and let stand for 5 minutes. Carve the chicken and serve.

Preheat the grill on high heat for 15 minutes. Turn 1 burner off and reduce the heat to medium on the remaining burners. Place the chicken over the burner that is off and close the lid. Grill for 45 minutes to 1 hour, or until cooked through completely. Turn once or twice while grilling.

POLYNESIAN GLAZED CHICKEN

SERVES 4

¼ c. extra virgin olive oil

3 green onions, finely minced

½ t. crushed red chili peppers

½ c. dry red wine

2 c. fresh orange juice

2 T. brown sugar

2 T. honey

3 to 4 lbs. roasting chicken, cut into serving portions

Mix together the oil, onions, chili peppers, wine, juice, sugar and honey. Grill the chicken as directed, basting often with the glaze.

Grill the chicken over medium coals for 25 to 30 minutes, basting often with the glaze. Turn and grill for 10 to 15 minutes, or until the chicken is cooked through completely. Continue glazing the chicken as it cooks.

Preheat the grill for 15 minutes on high heat. Turn 1 burner off and reduce the heat on the remaining burners to medium. Place the chicken, skin side up, over the burner that is off and close the lid. Grill the chicken for 40 to 50 minutes, basting often with the glaze. Turn the chicken after about 30 minutes to brown both sides.

SAGE-STUFFED CHICKEN BREASTS

SERVES 4

4 boneless chicken breasts

1 c. prepared herb stuffing mix

¼ c. yellow onion, chopped

¼ c. celery, chopped

1 t. ground sage

½ t. ground rosemary

Cut a deep horizontal cut in the middle of each chicken breast. Mix together the remaining ingredients and stuff into each breast. Grill as directed.

Grill the breasts over medium-hot coals for 10 minutes. Turn and continue grilling until cooked through completely, about 3 to 6 minutes.

Preheat the grill on high heat for 10 minutes. Grill the chicken on medium heat for 10 minutes; turn and continue grilling for 6 minutes or until cooked through completely.

WINE & HERB GRILLED CHICKEN

SERVES 4

1 c. canola oil

2 green onions, finely minced

½ t. salt

½ c. dry white wine

¼ c. fresh lemon juice

1 t. fresh rosemary, crushed

1 T. fresh parsley, minced

1 T. fresh thyme, minced

3 to 4 lb. roasting chicken, cut into serving portions

Mix together the oil, onions, salt, wine, lemon juice and herbs. Place the chicken in a large glass pan and cover with the marinade. Refrigerate for 2 hours or up to 10 hours. Grill the chicken as directed, basting often.

Grill the chicken over medium coals for 25 to 30 minutes, basting often with the marinade. Turn and grill for 10 to 15 minutes, or until the chicken is cooked through completely. Continue basting the chicken as it cooks.

Preheat the grill for 15 minutes on high heat. Turn 1 burner off and reduce the heat on the remaining burner(s) to medium. Place the chicken, skin side up, over the burner that is off and close the lid. Grill the chicken for 45 minutes to 1 hour, basting often with the marinade. Turn the chicken after about 30 minutes to brown both sides.

POBLANO CHICKEN QUESADILLAS

SERVES 4

½ t. garlic powder

½ t. ground chili powder

½ t. poblano chilies, minced

½ t. freshly ground black pepper

3 boneless chicken breasts

4 whole wheat soft tortillas

1½ c. pepper Jack cheese, shredded

¼ c. sour cream

2 green onions, minced

Mix together the garlic powder, chili powder, chilies and pepper and press the mixture into the chicken breasts on all sides. Grill as directed. Chop the grilled chicken into small pieces. To serve, place cheese on each tortilla and cover with cream, chicken and green onions. Fold in half and grill for 2 to 3 minutes, until cheese melts. Cut into wedges and serve.

Grill the chicken over medium coals for 6 minutes. Turn and continue grilling for 6 to 8 minutes, or until the chicken is cooked through completely.

Preheat the grill for 10 to 15 minutes on high heat. Reduce the heat to medium and grill the chicken for 12 to 14 minutes, or until cooked through completely.

SUPER BBQ CHICKEN
WITH HORSERADISH SAUCE

SERVES 4

1 T. prepared horseradish

½ c. yellow onion, diced

½ c. ketchup

¼ c. Worcestershire sauce

1 T. sugar

1 t. mustard powder

3 to 4 lbs. roasting chicken, cut into serving pieces

Mix together all ingredients except the chicken. Grill the chicken as directed, basting often with the barbecue sauce. Discard any remaining sauce.

Grill the chicken over medium coals for 15 to 25 minutes, basting often with the sauce. Turn and grill for 20 to 30 minutes, or until the chicken is cooked through completely. Continue basting the chicken as it cooks.

Preheat the grill for 15 minutes on high heat. Turn 1 burner off and reduce the heat on the remaining burner(s) to medium. Place the chicken, skin side up, over the burner that is off and close the lid. Grill the chicken for 45 minutes to 1 hour, basting every 15 minutes with the sauce. Turn the chicken after about 30 minutes to brown both sides.

PINEAPPLE & LIME GRILLED CHICKEN

SERVES 4

2 c. fresh or frozen, reconstituted pineapple juice

¼ c. fresh lime juice

¼ c. soy sauce

¼ c. vegetable oil

¼ c. honey

3 cloves garlic, minced

1 t. salt

½ t. ground black pepper

2 t. fresh cilantro, minced

3 to 4 lbs. roasting chicken, cut into serving pieces

Mix together in a large bowl the juices, soy sauce, oil, honey, garlic, salt, pepper and cilantro. Place the chicken in a large glass baking pan and pour the marinade over the chicken. Refrigerate for 2 or up to 12 hours. Grill the chicken as directed, basting often with the marinade.

Grill the chicken over medium coals for 15 to 25 minutes, basting often with the marinade. Turn and grill for 20 to 30 minutes, or until the chicken is cooked through completely. Continue basting the chicken as it cooks.

Preheat the grill for 15 minutes on high heat. Turn 1 burner off and reduce the heat on the remaining burner(s) to medium. Place the chicken, skin side up, over the burner that is off and close the lid. Grill the chicken for 45 minutes up to 1 hour, basting every 15 minutes with the marinade. Turn the chicken after about 30 minutes to brown both sides.

SWEET SOUTHERN BARBECUE CHICKEN

SERVES 4

¼ c. Worcestershire sauce

¼ c. butter, softened

1 c. ketchup

¼ c. water

1 small white onion, chopped

2 cloves garlic, minced

2 T. apple cider vinegar

3 T. dark brown sugar

3 T. molasses

2 t. chili powder

1 t. cayenne pepper

3 to 4 lbs. roasting chicken, cut
into serving pieces

Prepare the marinade by placing the Worcestershire sauce, butter and ketchup in a medium saucepan. Cook and stir over medium heat for 2 minutes; remove from the heat and add the remaining ingredients, except chicken. Mix well. Place the chicken in a large glass baking pan and pour the marinade over the chicken. Refrigerate for 2 or up to 12 hours. Grill the chicken as directed, basting often with the marinade.

Grill the chicken over medium coals for 15 to 25 minutes, basting often with the marinade. Turn and grill for 25 to 35 minutes, or until the chicken is cooked through completely. Continue basting the chicken as it cooks.

Preheat the grill for 15 minutes on high heat. Turn 1 burner off and reduce the heat on the remaining burner(s) to medium. Place the chicken, skin side up, over the burner that is off and close the lid. Grill the chicken for 45 minutes to 1 hour, basting every 15 minutes with the marinade. Turn the chicken after about 30 minutes to brown both sides.

TURKEY BREAST A LA FIESTA

SERVES 8

1 c. vegetable oil

¼ c. orange juice

¼ c. lime juice

2 t. chili powder

2 t. dried sage leaves, crushed

1 t. salt

½ t. freshly ground black pepper

3 to 4 lbs. boneless turkey breast

Mix together all ingredients except the turkey. Place the turkey in a large glass pan and pour the marinade over the turkey. Cover tightly and refrigerate for 1 hour or up to 12 hours. Turn the turkey breast often as it marinates. Grill as directed. Let stand 10 minutes before serving.

Grill the turkey breast, skin side down, over medium-hot coals for 6 to 8 minutes, or until the skin is golden and crisp. Turn and baste with some of the marinade. Arrange the coals slightly to reduce the heat and cover the turkey breast with aluminum foil. Grill for 40 to 50 minutes over medium coals or until the turkey is completely cooked through.

Preheat the grill for 15 minutes on high heat. Place the turkey breast, skin side down, on the grill and cook for 8 minutes. Turn and baste with the marinade. Cover the turkey with foil and close the lid. Reduce the heat to medium and grill for 45 to 55 minutes until cooked through completely.

TURKEY MEDALLIONS IN GINGER-ORANGE MARINADE

SERVES 6

6 boneless turkey medallions, about ¾-inch thick

1 c. orange juice

¼ c. molasses

2 t. fresh ginger, finely grated

4 cloves garlic

¼ c. canola oil

Place the turkey in a large, self-sealing plastic bag. Add the remaining ingredients and combine well. Refrigerate for at least 1 hour or up to 12 hours. Grill as directed.

Lightly oil the grids of the grill. Grill the turkey for 6 minutes over medium coals. Turn and grill for 6 to 8 minutes, or until cooked through completely.

Lightly oil the grill before heating. Preheat the grill for 10 to 15 minutes on high heat. Reduce the heat to medium and add the medallions. Close the lid and grill for 6 to 7 minutes. Turn and grill for 6 to 9 minutes, or until cooked through completely.

HERB-CRUSTED AHI TUNA STEAKS

SERVES 8

8 very fresh Ahi tuna steaks

½ c. extra virgin olive oil

¼ c. fresh cilantro, finely minced

¼ c. fresh chervil, finely minced

2 T. fresh parsley, finely minced

1 T. lemon peel, finely minced

2 cloves garlic, minced

1 t. salt

1 t. freshly ground black pepper

Place the steaks on a flat surface. Process the oil, herbs, lemon peel, garlic, salt and pepper in a food processor for 2 minutes. Pat the herb mixture evenly onto 1 side of each steak. Grill as directed.

Lightly oil the grill. Add the steaks and grill over medium coals for 4 minutes, herb side down. Turn and grill for 3 to 4 minutes for medium rare steaks, or as desired.

Lightly oil the grill. Preheat the grill for 10 to 15 minutes on high heat. Reduce the heat to medium and grill the steaks for 4 minutes, herb side down. Turn and grill for 4 to 8 minutes for medium-rare steaks, or as desired.

GRILLED HALIBUT IN TOMATO BASIL COULI

SERVES 6

Halibut steaks are mild, but hold good consistency when grilled. This tomato couli is a perfect foil to the mild fish.

2 oz. fresh basil, chopped

4 cloves garlic, chopped

1 T. fresh lemon juice

8 oz. can tomato sauce

2 plum tomatoes, chopped

1 t. ground black pepper

1 t. salt

2 T. extra virgin olive oil

6 halibut steaks, about 1-inch thick

fresh basil for garnish

Place all ingredients, except the fish and garnish, in a blender and pulse until smooth. Set aside. Grill the halibut steaks as directed. To serve, place a pool of the couli on each plate and top with the halibut steaks. Garnish with basil leaves, if desired.

Lightly oil the grill. Grill the halibut over medium coals for 3 minutes. Turn and continue grilling cooked to your preference.

Lightly oil the grill. Preheat the grill for 10 to 15 minutes on high heat. Reduce the heat to medium and turn off 1 burner. Place the steaks over the burner that is off and close the lid. Grill for 6 to 7 minutes. Turn and continue grilling until cooked to your preference.

SPICE-RUBBED SALMON FILLETS

SERVES 6

¼ t. ground cloves

¼ t. ground allspice

1 t. cayenne pepper

2 T. ground paprika

½ t. chili powder

1 t. ground black pepper

1 t. garlic powder

2 t. onion powder

2 t. seasoned salt

2 T. dark brown sugar

3 T. sugar

6 salmon fillets, 6 to 8 oz. each

Combine all ingredients, except the salmon, in a small bowl. Gently rub and press the mixture into each fillet, covering both sides. Let stand for 5 minutes. Grill as directed.

Lightly oil the grill. Grill the fish over medium coals for 5 minutes. Turn and grill for 5 to 8 minutes, or until cooked to your preference.

Oil the grill. Preheat the grill for 10 to 15 minutes on high heat. Turn off 1 burner and reduce the remaining burner(s) to medium heat. Place the fillets over the burner that is off and grill for 5 to 6 minutes. Turn and grill for 7 to 9 minutes, or until cooked to your preference.

COCONUT MARGARITA GRILLED TILAPIA

SERVES 4 TO 6

¼ c. orange-flavored liqueur

¼ c. coconut milk

2 T. gold tequila

¼ t. ground cinnamon

2 T. dark brown sugar

2 T. fresh lemon juice

½ t. salt

1½ to 2 lbs. tilapia fillets

shredded coconut for garnish

Mix together all of the ingredients except the tilapia. Place the fillets in a glass pan and pour the marinade over the fish. Cover tightly and refrigerate for 1 hour. Grill as directed. Sprinkle the coconut evenly over the fillets to serve.

Lightly oil the grill. Grill the fish over medium coals for 4 to 5 minutes. Turn and grill for 6 to 8 minutes, or until cooked to your preference.

Oil the grill. Preheat the grill for 10 to 15 minutes on high heat. Turn off 1 burner and reduce the remaining burner(s) to medium heat. Place the fillets over the burner that is off and grill for 6 to 8 minutes. Turn and grill for 6 to 8 minutes, or until cooked to your preference.

MUSTARD LEMON FILLET OF SOLE

SERVES 4

¼ c. white vinegar

1 T. fresh lemon juice

½ c. extra virgin olive oil

2 t. salt

1 t. garlic powder

1 t. ground black pepper

1 t. dry mustard

4 sole fillets, about 4 oz. each

lemon wedges for garnish

Combine all of the ingredients, except the fish and lemon wedges. Place the fillets in a large glass pan and cover with the marinade. Wrap tightly and refrigerate for 1 hour or up to 2 hours. Turn once while marinating. Grill as directed. Serve with lemon wedges.

Lightly oil the grill. Grill the fish over medium coals for 4 to 5 minutes. Turn and grill for 4 to 5 minutes, or until cooked to your preference.

Oil the grill. Preheat the grill for 10 to 15 minutes on high heat. Turn off 1 burner and reduce the remaining burner(s) to medium heat. Place the fillets over the burner that is off and grill for 4 to 5 minutes. Turn and grill for 4 to 5 minutes, or until cooked to your preference.

MEDITERRANEAN SWORDFISH

SERVES 8

¼ c. lemon juice

½ c. extra virgin olive oil

1 t. dried marjoram

1 T. lemon peel, grated

3 T. ketchup

1 t. salt

1 t. freshly ground black pepper

1 clove garlic, finely minced

2 lbs. swordfish fillets, cut into 1½ inch cubes

8 bamboo or metal skewers

Combine all of the ingredients, except the fish, in a bowl. Thread the fish onto each skewer. Grill as directed.

Lightly oil the grill. Grill the kebobs over medium coals for 6 to 8 minutes, brushing with the sauce once or twice. Turn the kebobs and brush with the sauce again. Grill for 6 to 7 minutes, or until cooked to your preference.

Oil the grill and preheat for 10 to 15 minutes on high heat. Turn off 1 burner and reduce the heat on the remaining burner(s) to medium. Grill the kebobs over the burner that is off for 7 to 9 minutes, brushing with the sauce occasionally. Turn and brush with the sauce again. Continue grilling for 7 to 8 minutes, or until cooked to your preference.

FRESH RASPBERRY GRILLED SEA BASS

SERVES 4

¼ c. fresh raspberries, washed and drained

¼ c. fresh lemon juice

½ c. extra virgin olive oil

½ t. dried Italian seasoning

½ t. salt

½ t. freshly ground black pepper

4 sea bass steaks, about ¾-inch in thickness

Place all of the ingredients, except the fish, in a blender and process until smooth. Place the steaks in a glass pan and cover with the marinade. Cover tightly and refrigerate for 1 hour. Grill as directed.

Lightly oil the grill. Add the steaks and grill over medium coals for 4 minutes. Turn and grill for 5 to 8 minutes, or until cooked to your preference.

Lightly oil the grill. Preheat the grill for 10 to 15 minutes on high heat. Reduce the heat to medium and grill the steaks for 5 minutes. Turn and grill for 6 to 8 minutes, or until cooked to your preference.

GRILLED FISH WITH BANANA MANGO SALSA

SERVES 6

¼ c. lime juice

2 T. fresh rosemary, crushed

¼ c. extra virgin olive oil

2 T. soy sauce

6 mild white fish fillets, about ½-inch thick

Banana Mango Salsa

1 large banana, cut into small pieces

1 large mango, cut into small pieces

½ honeydew melon, cut into small chunks

½ c. purple onion, chopped

1 ripe tomato, cut into small pieces

¼ c. fresh cilantro, finely minced

Combine the juice, rosemary, oil and soy sauce in a self-sealing plastic bag. Add the fillets and marinate for 1 hour. Grilled as directed and serve with the *Banana Mango Salsa*.

To prepare the *Banana Mango Salsa*, gently combine all ingredients in a serving bowl. Let stand prior to serving.

Lightly oil the grill. Grill the steaks over medium coals for 6 to 8 minutes, brushing with the marinade once or twice. Turn the steaks and brush with the marinade again. Grill for 6 minutes, or until cooked to your preference.

Oil the grill and preheat for 10 to 15 minutes on high heat. Turn off 1 burner and reduce the heat on the remaining burner(s) to medium. Grill the steaks over the burner that is off for 7 to 9 minutes, brushing with the marinade occasionally. Turn and brush with the marinade again. Continue grilling for 7 to 8 minutes, or until cooked to your preference.

GRILLED HALIBUT VERACRUZ

SERVES 4

4 halibut fillets, 6 oz. each

3 T. vegetable oil

1 T. ground paprika

1 t. ground black pepper

Veracruz Sauce

¼ c. canned green chilies, chopped

¼ c. pimento-stuffed green olives, sliced

¼ c. extra virgin olive oil

1 small onion, chopped

4 small plum tomatoes, chopped

1 cloves garlic, minced

¼ t. ground cinnamon

¼ t. ground cloves

½ t. brown sugar

2 T. fresh lime juice

1 t. salt

Place the fillets on a flat surface. Mix together the oil, paprika and pepper and smooth the mixture over both sides of each fillet. Grill as directed and serve with the *Veracruz Sauce.*

To prepare the *Veracruz Sauce,* sauté the green chilies and olives in the oil for 2 minutes over medium heat. Add the onion, tomatoes and garlic and sauté for 2 minutes. Add the remaining ingredients and heat for 2 minutes.

Lightly oil the grill. Add the steaks and grill over medium coals for 5 minutes. Turn and grill for 5 to 8 minutes, or until cooked to your preference.

Lightly oil the grill. Preheat the grill for 10 to 15 minutes on high heat. Reduce the heat to medium and grill the steaks for 5 minutes. Turn and grill for 6 to 9 minutes, or until cooked to your preference.

SALMON STEAKS
WITH PINEAPPLE TERIYAKI GLAZE

SERVES 4

1 c. hickory-flavored barbecue sauce

2 T. hoisin sauce

2 T. sesame oil

1 t. prepared mustard

1 t. ground ginger

2 cloves garlic, minced

2 T. dark brown sugar

2 c. canned or fresh pineapple chunks

4 salmon steaks, about 1-inch thick

Combine all ingredients, except the pineapple and fish, in a saucepan. Stir and cook over low heat until well-blended. Remove from the heat and cool for 5 minutes. Grill the steaks as directed, brushing the steaks with the glaze. To serve, heat the remaining glaze again and add the pineapple chunks. Cook over low heat for 3 minutes. Cover each grilled steak with generous portions of the pineapple and glaze.

Lightly oil the grill. Add the steaks and grill over medium coals for 6 minutes, brushing with the glaze once or twice. Turn and grill for 6 to 9 minutes, basting with the glaze again, or until cooked to your preference.

Lightly oil the grill. Preheat the grill for 10 to 15 minutes on high heat. Reduce the heat to medium and grill the steaks for 5 minutes. Brush the steaks with the glaze once or twice. Turn and brush the steaks with the glaze again. Grill for 6 to 10 minutes, basting occasionally, or until cooked to your preference.

GARLICKY GRILLED SHRIMP

SERVES 4

20 raw jumbo shrimp, shelled, deveined

¾ c. dry white wine

¼ c. vegetable oil

4 cloves garlic, finely minced

½ t. white pepper

¼ t. crushed red chilies

1 T. fresh cilantro, chopped

Place the shrimp in a large, self-sealing plastic bag and add the remaining ingredients. Marinate in the refrigerator for 1 hour. Grill as directed.

Lightly coat a seafood barbecue tray with oil. Discard the marinade and place the shrimp on the tray and grill over medium coals for 3 minutes. Turn once and grill for 2 to 3 minutes, or until the shrimp turn uniformly opaque.

Lightly coat a seafood barbecue tray with oil. Preheat the grill for 10 to 15 minutes on high heat. Discard the marinade and place the shrimp on the tray. Reduce the heat to medium and grill the shrimp for 3 minutes. Turn once and grill for 2 to 4 minutes, or until the shrimp turn uniformly opaque.

BUTTERY GRILLED SCALLOP KEBOBS

SERVES 4 TO 5

½ c. unsalted butter, melted

2 T. fresh parsley, minced

1 t. salt

½ t. white pepper

1½ to 2 lbs. sea scallops

8 to 10 bamboo or metal skewers

Combine the butter, parsley, salt and pepper in a small bowl. Thread the scallops onto the skewers. Grill as directed, basting with the sauce.

Lightly oil the grill. Grill kebobs over medium coals for 2 minutes, brushing with the sauce once or twice. Turn kebobs and brush with sauce again. Grill for 2 minutes, or until cooked completely through.

Oil the grill and preheat for 10 to 15 minutes on high heat. Turn off 1 burner and reduce the heat on the remaining burner(s) to medium. Grill the kebobs for 2 to 3 minutes over the burner that is off, brushing with the sauce occasionally. Turn and brush with the sauce again. Continue grilling for 2 minutes, or until cooked completely through.

CHILE-SEASONED GRILLED CORN

SERVES 4

6 T. butter, melted

1 clove garlic, minced

¼ t. crushed red chile pepper

½ t. freshly ground black pepper

1 t. salt

1 t. fresh parsley, minced

4 ears corn on the cob, husked

In a small bowl, blend all ingredients, except the corn. Set aside and grill corn as directed.

Over medium-hot coals, place the corn on an oiled grill. Cover and cook for 15 to 20 minutes, frequently turning the corn and brushing it with the butter sauce. The corn will be fork tender when ready to serve.

Preheat the grill on medium-high heat for 10 minutes. Reduce the heat to medium. Place the corn on the grill, cover and cook for 20 minutes, turning the corn frequently and basting with the butter sauce. The corn will be fork-tender when done.

GRILLED ROSEMARY POTATOES & ONIONS

SERVES 4

4 large russet potatoes

2 white onions, cut into wedges

4 T. butter, cut into T.

1 T. fresh basil, minced

1 T. fresh rosemary, minced

salt and black pepper to taste

Open each potato by cutting deeply into fourths. Do not cut completely through. Place each potato on a large piece of foil. Position the onions around the potatoes, top each with butter and cover with herbs, salt and pepper. Wrap tightly and grill as directed.

Cook the potato pockets on grill over medium-hot coals for 35 to 40 minutes, or until potatoes are tender. Remove and serve while hot.

Preheat the grill on high heat for 10 to 15 minutes. Place the pockets evenly on the grill. Reduce the heat to medium, cover the grill and cook for 45 minutes, or until potatoes are tender. Remove and serve while hot.

GRILL-ROASTED SWEET POTATOES

SERVES 4 GENEROUSLY

4 garnet yams, peeled and sliced thinly

¼ c. white onion, chopped

¼ c. butter, softened

½ t. seasoned salt

¼ t. black pepper

Prepare 4 large squares of foil. Place equal portions of potatoes and onion in the center of each square. Evenly divide the butter, seasoned salt and pepper over the potatoes and close the foil packets tightly. Grill the packets as directed.

Grill directly in or next to medium coals. Shift and turn the packets every 10 minutes or so, grilling about 40 minutes total. The potatoes will be soft and steaming when ready to serve. Remove the foil carefully.

POSOLE CHILI

SERVES 4

½ lb. beef hangar steak

2 t. vegetable oil

1 t. ground chili powder

Posole

2 c. cooked posole

½ t. liquid smoke

1 large yellow onion

2 c. canned pinto beans, drained

4 ripe tomatoes, chopped

15 oz. can tomato sauce

2 cloves garlic, minced

12 oz. Mexican beer

Grill the beef as directed. Combine the steak pieces with all of the remaining ingredients in a slow cooker and stir well to combine. Cook on Low for 6 to 8 hours or on High for 3 to 4 hours. Stir occasionally.

Grill the beef over medium-hot coals for 5 minutes and add the oil and powder. Continue grilling for 2 minutes. Let stand for 5 minutes; chop into bite-sized pieces.

Preheat the grill on medium-high for 10 minutes. Grill the steak for 5 minutes, turn and add the oil and powder. Continue grilling for 3 minutes. Let stand for 5 minutes; chop into bite-sized pieces.

GRILLED NAVAJO BREAD

SERVES 6

2 c. whole wheat flour

4 t. baking powder

1¼ c. whole milk

1 egg

2 T. vegetable oil

In a large bowl, mix the flour and baking powder. Add the milk and egg and stir with a spoon until the batter is spongy. Pour the oil into a cast iron skillet and turn to coat the bottom and sides of the pan. Heat the oil in the skillet over the grill. Spoon the bread batter into the skillet. Grill the bread as directed. To serve, pull pieces of the bread and enjoy with grilled meat and/or beans.

Place the skillet on the grill over medium-hot coals and cook for 15 minutes. When the bottom of the bread is brown, carefully turn the bread using 2 large spatulas. Grill again for about 15 minutes. Remove from the pan and cool slightly.

Preheat the grill for 15 minutes on high heat. Reduce the heat to medium and place the bread in the skillet on the rack. Close the lid. Grill for 15 to 20 minutes. Turn the bread using 2 large spatulas and grill for an additional 15 minutes. Remove from the pan and cool slightly.

GRILLED BALSAMIC VEGETABLES

SERVES 4 TO 6

1 red pepper, cut into 1-inch squares

1 yellow pepper, cut into 1-inch squares

2 zucchini squash, washed and cut into ¼-inch thick slices

18 cherry tomatoes, washed

1 large purple onion, thickly sliced

18 crimini mushrooms, scrubbed and trimmed

½ c. extra virgin olive oil

2 T. balsamic vinegar

1 t. freshly ground black pepper

½ t. salt

Toss the vegetables together in a large bowl. Mix together the oil, vinegar, pepper and salt and pour over the vegetables. Turn and toss the vegetables again to coat. Refrigerate for 1 hour, turning the vegetables every 15 minutes. Grill as directed.

Coat a perforated grilling tray with oil or cooking spray. Grill the vegetables over medium coals for 5 to 7 minutes, turning occasionally, until the vegetables are soft.

Preheat the grill for 10 to 15 minutes on high heat. Reduce the heat to medium. Place the vegetables in a perforated grilling tray and grill for 10 to 15 minutes with the lid closed, turning often.

ZESTY MARINATED ZUCCHINI

SERVES 3 TO 4

4 medium zucchini, sliced horizontally into 4 pieces each

1 c. garlic and cheese-flavored salad dressing

Parmesan cheese for garnish

Place the zucchini in a self-sealing bag and add the dressing. Chill for 1 hour. Discard the marinade and grill as directed. Cover lightly with the cheese before serving.

Grill the zucchini over medium coals for 5 minutes. Turn and grill for 2 minutes, until tender-crisp.

Preheat the grill for 10 minutes on high heat. Grill the zucchini on medium heat for 5 minutes. Turn and grill for 3 minutes, until tender-crisp.

GINGER OIL-GRILLED CARROTS

SERVES 4 TO 6

¼ c. vegetable oil

½ t. ground ginger

¼ t. salt

1 t. fresh parsley, minced

6 large carrots, peeled and ends trimmed

Blend the oil with the ginger, salt and parsley and set aside. Grill the carrots as directed, brushing with the ginger oil occasionally. To serve, cut the grilled carrots into slices about ½-inch in width and serve while warm.

Grill the whole carrots over medium coals for 4 minutes, brushing with the oil occasionally. Turn and grill for 2 to 3 minutes, or until soft. Brush again with the oil.

Preheat the grill for 10 to 15 minutes on high heat. Place the carrots on the grill and reduce the heat to medium. Brush with the oil and close the lid. Grill for 5 minutes. Turn the carrots and brush again with the oil. Grill for 3 to 4 minutes, or until the carrots are soft.

BARBECUED WHOLE GARLIC

SERVES 12

6 whole garlic bulbs

3 T. extra virgin olive oil

Lightly rub off any loose garlic skins. Cut the top of the bulbs off to expose each of the garlic heads inside. Sprinkle the cut side of each bulb with oil. Grill as directed. To serve, scoop the garlic from the bulbs and serve on Italian bread or flatbread.

Grill the bulbs, cut side down, over medium coals for 20 minutes, or until the bulbs are very soft.

Preheat the grill for 15 minutes on high heat. Reduce the heat to medium and turn off 1 burner. Place the bulbs over the burner that is off and close the lid. Grill for 20 to 30 minutes until the bulbs are very soft.

EASY MARINATED MUSHROOM & ARTICHOKE SKEWERS

SERVES 4 TO 6

2 - 8 oz. jars marinated artichokes, oil reserved

3 c. small button mushrooms

10 bamboo or metal skewers

Combine the artichokes and mushrooms with the oil in a large glass or plastic bowl. Cover tightly and refrigerate overnight. Turn the vegetables occasionally. Thread the mushrooms and artichoke pieces onto the skewers, alternating each. Grill as directed.

Grill the skewers over medium coals for 4 minutes. Turn and grill for 2 to 3 minutes or until the vegetables are browned and soft.

Preheat the grill for 10 to 15 minutes on high heat. Reduce the heat to medium and grill the vegetables for 4 to 5 minutes. Turn and grill for 2 to 3 minutes or until the vegetables are browned and soft.

GRILLED PORTOBELLOS WITH FRESH MOZZARELLA

SERVES 4

4 large portobello mushrooms, cleaned and dried

¼ c. extra virgin olive oil

1 t. freshly ground black pepper

1 t. salt

1 T. fresh lemon juice

4 slices fresh mozzarella cheese, about ⅛-inch thick

Place the mushrooms on a flat surface, stem side up. Sprinkle each with the oil, pepper, salt and lemon juice. Grill as directed.

Grill the mushrooms over medium coals for 8 minutes, with the stem side down. Turn and place 1 slice of cheese over each mushroom. Grill for 3 minutes or until the cheese has softened over the mushrooms.

Preheat the gas grill for 10 to 15 minutes on high heat. Reduce the heat to medium. Grill the mushrooms for 8 minutes, with the stem side down. Turn and place 1 slice of cheese over each mushroom. Grill for 3 minutes or until the cheese has softened over the mushrooms.

GRILLED SWEET & TENDER ONIONS

SERVES 6 TO 8

4 Vidalia onions, peeled and sliced ¼-inch thick

¼ c. extra virgin olive oil

2 T. fresh thyme, finely minced

1 t. salt

1 t. freshly ground black pepper

Place the whole slices on a flat surface. Sprinkle each with the olive oil, thyme, salt and pepper. Grill as directed.

Grill the onion slices over medium coals for 3 min. Turn and grill for 2 to 3 minutes, or until soft.

Preheat the grill for 10 to 15 minutes on high heat. Reduce the heat to medium and place the onion slices on the grill. Cook for 4 minutes. Turn and grill for 2 to 3 minutes or until soft.

GRILLED ROSEMARY POLENTA
WITH GOAT CHEESE

SERVES 6 TO 8

8 c. chicken broth

2 c. finely ground yellow cornmeal

½ t. salt

¼ c. goat cheese, softened

2 T. olive oil

½ t. freshly ground black pepper

sprigs fresh rosemary, crumbled

Butter the sides and bottom of a 9 by 13-inch baking dish. Heat the chicken broth in a large stockpot to a boil and slowly add the cornmeal. Whisk constantly after each small addition. Reduce the heat to low and cook until thickened, about 15 minutes. Fold in the salt, goat cheese, oil and pepper and pour into the baking dish. Cover tightly with plastic wrap and refrigerate overnight. Cut the polenta into small squares and brush with olive oil and a few crumbles of the rosemary. Grill as directed.

Grill the polenta squares over medium coals for 2 minutes. Turn and continue grilling for 2 to 3 minutes, until golden brown.

Preheat the grill for 10 to 15 minutes on high heat. Reduce the heat to medium and grill the polenta squares for 3 minutes. Turn and grill for 3 minutes, or until golden brown.

SLOW-GRILLED BAJA BEANS

SERVES 8

2 c. navy beans

1 yellow onion, chopped

2 plum tomatoes, chopped

2 cloves garlic, minced

3 T. dark molasses

1 t. dry mustard

¼ c. canned green chilies, chopped

1 t. chili powder

Soak the beans overnight in water to cover. Drain and cover the beans with fresh water in a large saucepan. Simmer the beans over low heat for 1 hour or until tender. Drain the beans again. Combine all of the remaining ingredients in a cast-iron Dutch oven and add the beans. Mix well. Grill as directed.

Place the Dutch oven on the grill and grill over medium-low heat for 2 hours, stirring often, or until full-flavored and hot throughout.

TRI-PEPPER POTATO SALAD

SERVES 6 TO 8

A sunny tribute to warm weather!

2 lbs. red potatoes, scrubbed and cut into cubes

¼ c. purple onion, minced

½ red bell pepper, chopped

½ green bell pepper, chopped

½ yellow bell pepper, chopped

2 cloves garlic, minced

½ c. prepared mayonnaise

3 T. fresh lime juice

1 t. freshly ground black pepper

pinch chili powder

¼ c. fresh cilantro, minced

Cut a large square of foil and arrange the potatoes and peppers on it. Cover with the garlic and another square of foil. Seal tightly and grill as directed. In a large serving bowl, combine all of the remaining ingredients and mix well. Add the grilled potatoes and combine again.

Grill vegetables on medium heat for 20 to 30 minutes until tender. Add to recipe as directed.

Preheat the grill for 10 to 15 minutes on high heat. Grill vegetable packet for 30 minutes, until tender. Add to recipe as directed.

ASIAN STEAK SALAD WITH WILD GREENS

SERVES 6

Garlic Soy Dressing

¾ c. vegetable oil

¼ c. soy sauce

2 cloves garlic, minced

3 green onions, chopped

1 t. ground ginger

2 T. clover honey

1½ lbs. beef flank steak

Salad:

8 c. mixed wild greens

1 cucumber, chopped

1 carrot, thinly sliced

¼ c. peanut oil

1 T. Asian sesame oil

½ t. Asian chile oil

3 T. rice wine vinegar

½ t. sugar

½ c. thin crispy noodles

To prepare the steak, combine the oil, soy sauce, garlic, green onions, ginger and honey in a self-sealing plastic bag. Add the steak, seal and chill for 12 hours. Grill as directed. Slice thinly across the grain.

To prepare the salad, toss the greens in a salad bowl. Add the vegetables. Whisk together the oils, vinegar and sugar and pour over the salad. Add the steak and toss lightly. Scatter the noodles over all before serving.

Grill the steak over medium coals for 20 to 25 minutes, or until cooked to medium-rare. Turn once while grilling.

Preheat the grill for 10 to 15 minutes on high heat. Reduce the heat to medium and place the steak on the grill. Close the lid and grill for 20 minutes. Turn and grill for 10 minutes, or until cooked to medium-rare.

CHICKEN, APRICOT & WALNUT WILD RICE

SERVES 4

2 small boneless chicken
breasts, grilled

½ c. celery, chopped

1 c. white onion, finely chopped

2 T. extra virgin olive oil

1⅔ c. wild rice

1 c. dry white wine

1½ c. water

1 t. fresh parsley, chopped

½ c. dried apricots, finely
chopped

½ c. raisins, finely chopped

¼ c. walnuts, finely chopped

1 t. fresh sage, minced

Thinly slice the chicken and chill. Preheat the oven to 350°F. Lightly coat a 2-quart baking dish with cooking spray and set aside. Sauté the celery and onion in the oil in a medium saucepan for 2 minutes. Pour the vegetables into the baking dish and add the rice, wine, water, parsley, apricots, raisins, walnuts and sage. Mix well. Cover and bake for 1 hour, stirring every 15 minutes. To serve, add the chicken, fluff the rice and garnish with additional walnuts, if desired.

PINEAPPLE & TOASTED SESAME BEEF SALAD

SERVES 4

A simple salad to complement any grilled entrée. This is especially good with Asian grilled beef or chicken.

2 T. sesame seeds

2 T. sesame seed oil

¼ c. rice vinegar

½ c. pineapple juice

10 c. romaine lettuce, shredded

¼ c. bean sprouts, cleaned and
cut into 1-inch pieces

1 carrot, peeled and grated

1 c. canned mandarin orange
segments, drained

½ lb. tenderloin steak, grilled,
thinly sliced

Pour the sesame seeds into a saucepan and toast until golden, about 2 minutes. Mix the seeds with the oil, vinegar and juice and whisk well. Combine the lettuce, sprouts, carrot and oranges in a serving bowl. Top with the steak slices. Pour the dressing over the salad and serve.